Chambers

# My First Picture Dictionary

hachette INDIA

First published in India in 2024 by Hachette India
(Registered name: Hachette Book Publishing India Pvt. Ltd)
An Hachette UK Company
www.hachetteindia.com
Chambers® is a registered trademark of Chambers Harrap Publishers Ltd,
an Hachette UK company

1



Text compiled and edited by Sunita Nahar

Layout, design and inside illustrations by Sonali Banerjee Mondol



ISBN 978-93-5731-383-4

Hachette Book Publishing India Pvt. Ltd
4th/5th Floors, Corporate Centre,
Plot No. 94, Sector 44, Gurugram 122003, India

FSC www.fsc.org MIX Paper | Supporting responsible forestry FSC® C010615

Printed and bound in India by
Thomson Press india Ltd.

# Foreword

Daljit Duck, Raju Rabbit, and Oscar Octopus have come together in this book to help young children discover and explore key vocabulary associated with the world around them. Children will enjoy exploring the mix of exciting animal and human characters, who strive to teach children everyday vocabulary through their fun-filled daily activities.

This my-first picture dictionary enriches language skills in young children through the collection of useful headwords and sentences to help explain the meaning of many memorable words.

Connecting pictures and words is a fundamental aspect of supporting early language and literacy skills in children. The dictionary format also helps to cultivate an understanding of reference books, which can in turn support independent learning as children grow and develop.

The book can be used in three phases of early learning. Firstly, to introduce fundamental words through brightly coloured pictures. Secondly, using guided sentences to provide meaning and context to the new vocabulary and finally, the book can be used over and over again to support independence when reading. **Chambers My First Picture Dictionary** is also a handy tool for teaching the spellings of essential words.

The thoughtfully crafted illustrations have a global appeal. The book will capture children's imagination and curiosity, supporting them to grow in confidence with early vocabulary. This charming **My First Picture Dictionary** is a must have for both home and classroom learning.

– Dr Karen Davison, Ulster University

**Living beings**

**Non-living objects**

# We are waiting inside the book!

One, two, three … where are we? Look us up inside the book, and write the page numbers where you found us.

**aeroplane:** Dexter Dog learns to fly an **aeroplane**.

**airport:** Dexter Dog flies down to the **airport**.

**alphabet:** A, the first letter of the **alphabet**, also means 'one'.

# Aa

**ambulance:** The **ambulance** is outside the clinic.

**angel:** The **angel** is dancing in the clouds.

**animals:** Squirrels are furry **animals** with bushy tails.

**ants:** **Ants** work hard all day.

**apple:** A crunchy green **apple** dropped from the tree.

**apron:** Poppy Panda has a pretty green **apron**.

**arrow:** The **arrow** has flown into the tree.

**astronaut:** Avril, the **astronaut**, has a white spacesuit.

# Bb

**baby:** The happy **baby** lies on the rug.

**badge:** Gertrude Giraffe wears a blue **badge**.

**bag:** The **bag** is full of warm clothes.

**baker:** Esther, the **baker**, is proud of her bread.

**ball:** Farookh Frog jumps over the **ball**.

a b c d e f g h i j k l m n o p q r s t u v w x y z

**balloon:** Madhu Mouse is carried away by the **balloon**.

**bananas:** The **bananas** are ready to be eaten.

**band:** The animal **band** has a blast.

**basket:** Oscar Octopus hates the **basket** full of smelly fish.

# Bb

**beans:** I love baked **beans**.

**bat:** Raju Rabbit is holding a cricket **bat**.

**bathtub:** Himani Hippo is in the **bathtub**.

**bear:** Babu Bear is a honey **bear**.

**bed:** Zamil Zebra is asleep in **bed**.

# Bb

**bee:** The **bee** smells the flower.

**bell:** Madhu Mouse is holding a **bell**.

**belt:** Babu Bear is wearing a big **belt**.

**bicycle:** Maisie Monkey has a new **bicycle**.

**bird:** Bill the **Bird** is talking to the chicks.

**blowing:** **Blowing** out birthday candles is hard.

**boat:** Oscar Octopus is alone in the **boat**.

**bone:** Dexter Dog is chewing a big **bone**.

a b c d e f g h i j k l m n o p q r s t u v w x y z

**book:** Warner Worm loves reading a **book**.

**boots:** **Boots** are made for walking.

**bottle:** A **bottle** of orange juice.

**bottom:** Maisie Monkey slides to the **bottom**.

# Bb

**bowl:** Babu Bear is holding a **bowl** of berries.

**box:** Coco Cat is curling up in a **box**.

**boy:** The **boy** loves his cat.

**branch:** Two birds are sitting on the **branch**.

**bread:** Madhu Mouse is eating the **bread**.

abcdefghijklmnopqrstuvwxyz

**breakfast:** **Breakfast** is laid out.

**brick:** Raju Rabbit is taking the **brick** home.

**bridge:** The boat is passing under the **bridge**.

# Bb

**brushing:** Larry Lion is **brushing** his mane.

**bubble:** Gogo Goat is making blue **bubbles**.

**bucket:** Farookh Frog is hiding under the **bucket**.

**building:** Babloo Bull is **building** a home.

**bull:** A **bull** has two horns.

**bulldozer:** Daljit Duck is pushing sand with a **bulldozer**.

# Bb

**bus:** The **bus** is standing outside the station.

**bush:** The **bush** is very green.

**butcher:** The **butcher** is holding the meat.

**butter:** Madhu Mouse loves to eat **butter**.

**butterfly:** A **butterfly** has colourful wings.

# Cc

**cabbage:** A tortoise should not eat **cabbage**.

**cage:** The tiger is locked in a **cage**.

**cake:** That's a yummy birthday **cake**!

**camel:** Daljit Duck is chatting with a **camel**.

**camera:** Bella the Elephant is using a **camera**.

**camping:** Dexter Dog is **camping** in the garden.

# Cc

**candle:** The cake has only one **candle**.

**car:** Daljit Duck has a shiny yellow sports **car.**

**cap:** Raju Rabbit loves his green sporty **cap**.

**carpet:** Coco has a favourite **carpet**.

**carrot:** Raju Rabbit bites into a **carrot**.

**castle:** This is a grand **castle**.

**cat:** Shh! Don't wake up Coco **Cat**.

**catching:** Raju Rabbit is **catching** the ball.

**caterpillar:** The green **caterpillar** has spots.

# Cc

**cave:** Scary creatures are hiding in this **cave**.

**chair:** Farookh Frog is resting on the **chair**.

**cauliflower:** Gogo Goat is eating the leaves of the **cauliflower**.

**chasing:** Coco Cat has not stopped **chasing** the mouse.

# Cc

**cheese:** Madhu Mouse makes holes in the **cheese**.

**cherries:** The red **cherries** are ripe.

**chicken:** Now the **chicken** will hatch her egg.

**chocolate:** The little girl loves **chocolate**.

**children:** The **children** are in the park

**chimney:** Santa is stuck in the **chimney**.

**Christmas:** Oscar Octopus has eight **Christmas** presents.

**church:** The **church** is very old.

**circle:** The ducks are making a **circle**.

**cleaning:** Shama Sheep has been **cleaning** all day.

**climbing:** Maisie Monkey doesn't like **climbing**.

**clock:** The cuckoo **clock** tells the time.

# Cc

**cloud:** The aeroplane is flying through the **cloud**.

**clown:** The **clown** has a big smile.

**coat:** Babu Bear is wearing a new **coat**.

**comb:** Larry Lion **combs** his whiskers every day.

**comic:** The **comic** tells stories in pictures.

**computer:** Maisie Monkey plays games on the **computer**.

**cook:** Shama Sheep loves to **cook** for Babu.

**counting:** Grandpa is **counting** coins.

**cow:** The calf licks his mother, the **cow**.

**cowboy:** Raju Rabbit wants to be a **cowboy**.

**crab:** This **crab** loves the sandy beach.

**crane:** Bella the Elephant is hanging from the **crane**.

**crashing:** The truck is **crashing** into the car.

**crayon:** Madhu Mouse is drawing an apple with a **crayon.**

**crocodile:** The old **crocodile** needs a walking stick.

**crossing:** The cars stopped at the zebra **crossing**.

**crown:** The king always wears his **crown**.

# Cc

**cry:** A crocodile can **cry** too!

**cucumber:** Raju Rabbit likes **cucumber** for snacks.

**cup:** Grandma is drinking tea from her new **cup**.

**curtain:** That's a beautiful yellow **curtain**.

**cutting:** Gogo Goat is **cutting** the stems.

a b c d e f g h i j k l m n o p q r s t u v w x y z

# Dd

**daffodils:** **Daffodils** grow in spring.

**dancer:** Shama Sheep is a ballet **dancer**.

**dancing:** Shama Sheep is **dancing** beautifully with Gogo Goat.

**dark:** Can you see the owl in the **dark**?

**deep:** Look at the lovely **deep** sea plants!

**deer:** This **deer** roams in the forest.

**dentist:** The **dentist** is checking Bella the Elephant's teeth.

**desert:** It is very hot in the **desert**.

# Dd

**desk:** Writer Rachel is writing at her **desk**.

**digging:** Dexter Dog is **digging** for his bone.

**dinosaur:** This green **dinosaur** eats everything.

**diving:** Farookh Frog loves **diving** into the sea.

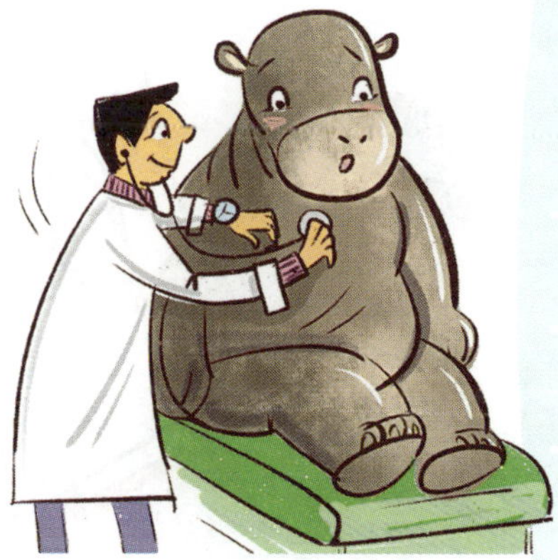

**doctor:** The **doctor** is checking Himani Hippo.

**dog:** Dexter **Dog** needs a bath.

**doll:** This is my favourite **doll**.

**dolphin:** The **dolphin** is playing in the water.

**door:** Oh no, Bella, don't pull the **door** – just knock on it.

**doughnut:** Mummy has made a **doughnut**.

**dragon:** A fiery **dragon** is flying in the air.

# Dd

**drawing:** The little boy is **drawing** a monkey.

**driving:** **Driving** a car on this road is difficult.

**dress:** Shama Sheep shows off her **dress**.

**drinking:** Tina loves **drinking** fruit juice.

**drum:** Babu Bear is playing a **drum**.

**duck:** Daljit **Duck** is gardening.

a b c d **e** f g h i j k l m n o p q r s t u v w x y z

**eagle:** An **eagle** is a bird of prey.

**earth:** We live on the **earth**.

**eating:** Babu Bear is **eating** bread and honey.

**egg:** This bird has hatched from an **egg**.

# Ee

**elephant:** Bella the **Elephant** is ready for the party.

**envelope:** Coco Cat is holding a green **envelope**.

**escalator:** Kiera Kangaroo is scared of the **escalator**.

a b c d e f g h i j k l m n o p q r s t u v w x y z

# Ee

**escaping:** The thief is **escaping**.

**exercising:** Himani Hippo is **exercising** every week.

# Ff

**factory:** Father works in a **factory**.

**fairy:** This is a beautiful **fairy**.

**falling:** Maisie Monkey is **falling** down.

**family:** Larry Lion has a big **family**.

**farmer:** The **farmer** has a sickle in his hand.

**father:** Larry Lion is **father** to little lion cubs.

**feather:** There is a **feather** in Raju Rabbit's hat.

**fence:** Sparky, the squirrel, leaps onto the **fence**.

**field:** The sheep have gathered in the **field**.

# Ff

**filling:** Babloo Bull is **filling** the tub.

**fire engine:** Don't worry! The **fire engine** has arrived.

**fishing:** Coco Cat is **fishing** for trout.

**flag:** Zamil Zebra is holding a colourful **flag**.

a b c d e f g h i j k l m n o p q r s t u v w x y z

**floating:** Five green leaves are **floating** in the pool.

**flower:** A beautiful **flower** for you!

**fly:** The **fly** is buzzing round my head.

# Ff

**fork:** Maisie Monkey has learned to eat with a **fork**.

**fountain:** Babu Bear is drinking from the **fountain**.

**fox:** The **fox** is peeping inside the hut.

**frog:** Farookh **Frog** is keeping his mouth shut.

**fruit:** Eating **fruit** is good for you.

a b c d e f **g** h i j k l m n o p q r s t u v w x y z

**game:** Warner Worm got this **game** on his birthday!

**garage:** Grandma is parking the car in the **garage**.

**garden:** Shama Sheep adores her **garden**.

**gate:** Farookh Frog jumps over the yellow **gate**.

# Gg

**ghost:** Himani Hippo is pretending to be a **ghost**.

**giant:** This **giant** is bigger than the house.

**giraffe:** Gertrude **Giraffe** has a long neck.

a b c d e f **g** h i j k l m n o p q r s t u v w x y z

# Gg

**girl:** This **girl** is skipping her rope.

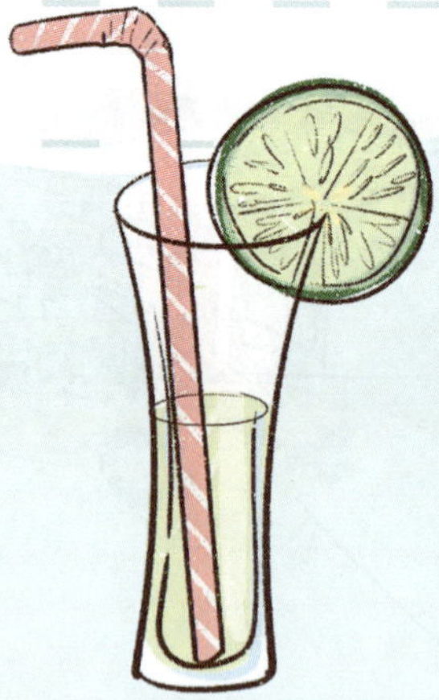

**glass:** Is the **glass** half full or half empty?

**glasses:** Warner Worm cannot read without his **glasses**.

**glove:** Puchku Penguin is wearing **gloves**.

**goose:** Mother **goose** has lots of chicks.

**goat:** The **goat** has stolen Shama Sheep's grocery bag.

**gold:** A **gold** necklace.

**gorilla:** This is a big, hairy **gorilla**.

**grapes:** A bowl of **grapes**.

# Gg

**grapefruit:** Babu Bear is going to have **grapefruit** for lunch.

**grass:** Tony Tiger is resting in the **grass**.

**grasshopper:** The **grasshopper** is as green as the grass.

**ground:** Who made this tunnel under the **ground**?

**group:** This **group** of monkeys is from the same family.

**guitar:** Kiera Kangaroo can play the **guitar**.

# Hh

**hammer:** A **hammer** is used for driving in nails.

**hamster:** This **hamster** is dancing with Madhu Mouse.

**handkerchief:** Cover your mouth and nose with a **handkerchief** when you cough or sneeze.

**hanging:** Maisie Monkey is **hanging** from the branch.

**hat:** Babu Bear has a lovely **hat**.

# Hh

**hedge:** The ball went over the **hedge**.

**helicopter:** The **helicopter** is landing.

**helmet:** Daljit Duck is wearing a **helmet**.

**helping:** Madhu Mouse is **helping** Coco Cat hang the clothes.

**hiding:** Look who's **hiding** in the tree!

# Hh

**hill:** Raju Rabbit is climbing the **hill**.

**hippopotamus:** Himani Hippo, the **hippopotamus**, is dancing the hula.

**holiday:** Shama Sheep is going on a summer **holiday**.

**honey:** Who spilled the **honey**?

**hook:** I hung my coat on this **hook**!

**horse:** There goes a brown **horse**.

**hospital:** Look who's come to see you in **hospital**.

**house:** A lovely wooden **house**!

# Ii

**ice:** Farookh Frog cracked the **ice**.

**insect:** Look at the **insect** – it's scary!

**iron:** You can press clothes with this **iron**.

**ice cream:** Kiera Kangaroo is licking the **ice cream**.

**island:** An **island** far away!

# Jj

**jacket:** Babu Bear is wearing a brand new **jacket**.

**jar:** The **jar** is not empty yet.

# Jj

**jeans:** Babu Bear is hanging his **jeans** on the washing line.

**jeep:** This green **jeep** has big wheels.

**jewels:** Shama Sheep loves **jewels**.

**jug:** A **jug** of lemonade.

**jumping:** Farookh Frog is **jumping** over the hurdle.

**jungle:** The **jungle** is home to these animals.

# Kk

**kangaroo:** Kiera **Kangaroo** lives in Australia.

**kettle:** This **kettle** makes a nice cup of tea.

**key:** Who put the **key** in the hole?

**kicking:** Raju Rabbit is **kicking** the football.

**king:** The **king** is sleepy.

# Kk

**kissing:** Katy is **kissing** her little dolly.

**kitchen:** Shama Sheep is cooking in the **kitchen**.

**kite:** Flying a **kite** is fun!

**knife**: Madhu Mouse is using a **knife** to slice the cake.

a b c d e f g h i j k **l** m n o p q r s t u v w x y z

**ladder:** Maisie Monkey wants to climb the **ladder**.

**lamb:** Lizzie **Lamb** is going home.

**lamp:** Himani Hippo is turning off the **lamp**.

**laughing:** Raju Rabbit can't help **laughing**.

# Ll

**leaf:** Farookh Frog finds shade under the **leaf**.

**lemon:** That's a yummy **lemon**.

**letter:** Shama Sheep is writing a **letter**.

**lettuce:** **Lettuce** is healthy.

# Ll

**lion:** Larry **Lion** is dreaming of food all day long.

**lizard:** A **lizard** loves eating flies.

**lighthouse:** That's a beautiful **lighthouse**.

**lollipop:** Splat, splat, slurp slurp, that is a lovely **lollipop**!

# Mm

**magician:** The **magician** pulls a rabbit from the hat.

**man:** This **man** is holding a briefcase.

**map:** Can you read the **map**?

**marbles:** These **marbles** roll well.

**mask:** Raju Rabbit is wearing a scary **mask**.

**matches:** Do not play with **matches**!

# Mm

**meat:** Where do you buy **meat**?

**medicine:** The baby does not like **medicine**.

**milk:** Coco Cat knocked over a bowl of **milk**.

**mirror:** Shama Sheep admires herself in the **mirror**.

**mobile:** Daljit Duck has a brand new **mobile**.

**money:** Ah, that's a lot of **money**!

**monkey:** Maisie is a cheeky **monkey**.

**moon:** The **moon** comes out at night.

# Mm

**mother:** Maisie Monkey is a proud **mother**.

**mountain:** I love to holiday in the **mountains**.

**mouse:** Madhu is a **mouse** with a curly tail.

**mug:** Daljit Duck is drinking milk from this **mug**.

**mushroom:** Farookh Frog is climbing onto the **mushroom**.

**nails:** Watch out! The **nails** are sharp and pointy.

**necklace:** Shama Sheep is wearing a beautiful **necklace**.

**needle:** Madhu Mouse is trying to thread a **needle**.

**nest:** These birds hatched in the **nest**.

# Nn

**net:** Babu Bear has a fish in his **net**.

**newspaper:** Babu Bear needs glasses to read the **newspaper**.

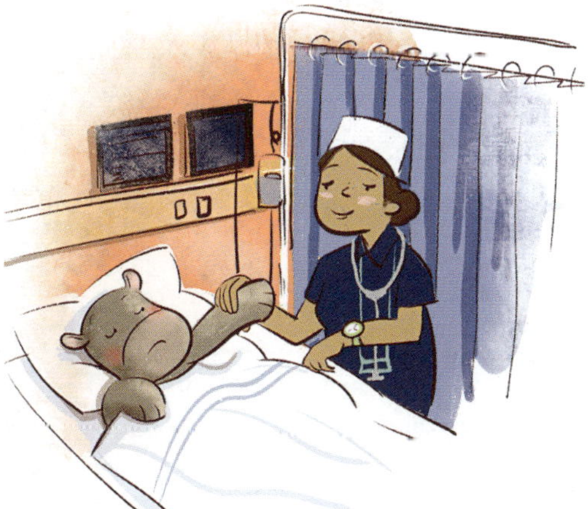

**nurse:** The **nurse** is taking care of Himani Hippo.

**nuts:** Sparky Squirrel is storing **nuts** for winter.

a b c d e f g h i j k l m n o p q r s t u v w x y z

# Oo

**octopus:** Oscar **Octopus** loves to gargle.

**office:** Warner Worm is dozing off in his **office**.

**onion:** The **onion** bulb has many skins.

**open:** **Open** sesame!

**orange:** Gogo Goat is eating a juicy **orange**.

**ostrich:** The **ostrich** loves to kick the ball.

**owl:** The **owl** is eying a rat.

# Pp

**painting:** Tony Tiger is at a **painting** workshop.

**pancake:** Shama Sheep is eating a **pancake**.

**panda:** Poppy **Panda** is eating bamboo.

**parachute:** Daljit Duck is landing with a **parachute**.

**park:** People love to spend time in the **park**.

**parrot:** This is a talking **parrot**.

**party:** **Party** time!

**paying:** Grandma is **paying** for the ball.

**peach:** A ripe, juicy **peach** ready to eat.

**pears:** Rinki loves to eat **pears**.

**peas:** Madhu Mouse has a tray of **peas**.

**pencil:** This is a **pencil**.

# Pp

**penguin:** Puchku **Penguin** wants a playmate.

**photograph:** This is a family **photograph**.

**piano:** The queen is learning to play the **piano**.

**picking:** Harry Hamster is **picking** blackberries.

**picnic:** Babu Bear and Maisie Monkey are having a **picnic**.

**pie:** Simple Simon dropped his **pie** on the road.

**pigeon:** The **pigeon** is sitting on the AC.

# Pp

**pillow:** That's a fun **pillow** fight.

**pineapple:** It's not easy to peel a **pineapple**.

**pin:** A **pin** is used to fasten clothes.

**pirate:** The police nabbed the cruel **pirate**.

abcdefghijklmnopqrstuvwxyz

**pit:** The little birdie is playing in the sand **pit**.

**pizza:** This **pizza** has lots of yummy cheese.

**planting:** Shama Sheep is **planting** a green vegetable.

# Pp

**plate:** Who served the crane soup on a **plate**?

**playing:** Kiera Kangaroo loves **playing** hopscotch.

**pockets:** That pair of cargoes has six **pockets**.

**poppy:** A beautiful red **poppy**.

**postwoman:** Shama Sheep is a **postwoman**.

a b c d e f g h i j k l m n o p q r s t u v w x y z

**potatoes: Potatoes** can be made into chips.

**present:** Larry Lion has received a **present**.

**princess:** This **princess** lives in a castle.

**pulling:** Maisie Monkey is **pulling** Himani Hippo's tail.

# Pp

**puppet:** A **puppet** looks like a human.

**puppy:** This is a newborn **puppy**.

**pram:** Shama Sheep has a **pram** full of lambs.

**pushing:** Why are you **pushing** me?

# Qq

**quarter:** You can have a **quarter** of the pizza.

**queen:** The **queen** loves to play football.

# Rr

**rabbit:** Raju is a white **rabbit**.

**racing:** Himani Hippo is driving a **racing** car.

**radiator:** The **radiator** makes the room warm.

**rain:** The peacock is enjoying the **rain**.

a b c d e f g h i j k l m n o p q **r** s t u v w x y z

**rainbow:** A **rainbow** has seven colours.

**rat:** A **rat** is bigger than a mouse.

**reading:** Ankur is **reading** a book.

**record:** Zamil Zebra is dancing to the **record**.

# Rr

**reindeers:** Female **reindeers** have antlers.

**ribbon:** A girl is tying a **ribbon** in her hair.

**riding:** Mr Croc is **riding** a tricycle.

**ring:** Shama Sheep is giving a **ring** to Oscar Octopus.

**river:** Fish spend all their time in the **river**.

**road:** Daljit Duck is skipping down the **road**.

**robot:** Wow! That's a flying **robot**!

# Rr

**rock:** Farookh Frog is sitting on the **rock**.

**rocket:** This **rocket** i going to Mars.

**rocking:** Madhu Mouse is riding her **rocking** horse.

**rolling:** Grandpa is **rolling** the snow into a ball.

**roof:** There's a cat on a hot tin **roof**.

# Rr

**rope:** The **rope** is breaking.

**roses:** Shama Sheep has a bunch of **roses**.

**rowing:** Gertrude Giraffe is **rowing** a boat.

**ruler:** A **ruler** is for measuring.

**running:** Haru Hare is **running** against Taru Tortoise.

# Ss

**sailor:** Dexter Dog has become a **sailor**.

**sand:** The camel can walk easily on **sand**.

# Ss

**sandals:** Gogo Goat is wearing **sandals** in the sun.

**sandwich:** That's a tuna **sandwich**.

**sausages:** Gablu Gibbon is eating **sausages**.

**saw:** A **saw** is for cutting wood.

**scarecrow:** A **scarecrow** stands in the garden.

**school:** Maisie Monkey is at **school**.

**scissors:** Bella the Elephant is cutting banana leaves with **scissors**.

**sea:** The dolphin is dancing in the **sea**.

**seal:** A **seal** eats fish.

**sewing:** Madhu Mouse is **sewing** a dress.

**shadow:** Coco Cat is watching her **shadow**.

**sheep:** Shama **Sheep** has a little lamb.

# Ss

**shell:** A **shell** is lying on the beach.

**ship:** This **ship** travels far and wide.

**shirt:** Bashir Buffalo is wearing a bright **shirt**.

**shoes:** A shoemaker is making new **shoes**.

a b c d e f g h i j k l m n o p q r s t u v w x y z

**shopping:** Zamil Zebra has gone **shopping**.

**shorts:** Kiera Kangaroo is wearing **shorts**.

**shouting:** The crow is **shouting** at Dexter Dog.

**shower:** Gopi Gorilla is having a **shower**.

# Ss

**signpost:** The camel is looking at the **signpost**.

**sink:** A big, blue fish is in the **sink**.

**skates:** Gertrude Giraffe has a new pair of **skates**.

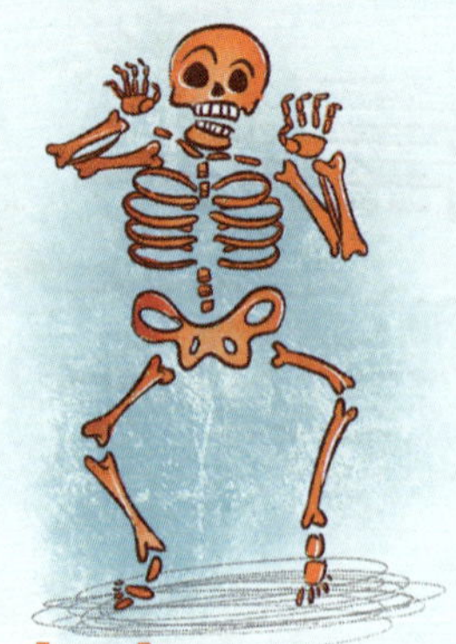

**skeleton:** A scary **skeleton**.

**skiing:** Tony Tiger has gone **skiing**.

**sleeping:** Grandpa is **sleeping** in his bedroom.

**slide:** A **slide** is for sliding down.

**slippers:** The tortoise wears his **slippers** at night.

# Ss

**smelling:** Zamil Zebra is **smelling** a red rose.

**snail:** A **snail** can live on the land.

**snake:** A creepy, poisonous **snake**.

**snow:** Do penguins get a cold in the **snow**?

**snowman:** Sparky Squirrel has made a tiny **snowman**.

**soap:** You wash your hands with **soap**.

**socks:** Five pairs of **socks** on the washing line.

**soldier:** The **soldier** is saving a little boy.

**spade:** Whose **spade** is this?

**spider:** Don't be scared of a **spider**.

**splashing:** Dexter Dog is **splashing** water on his face.

**spoon:** You can't eat a sandwich with a **spoon**.

**squirrel:** Sparky is a very pretty **squirrel**.

**stairs:** These **stairs** go up to the bedroom.

**stamp:** There is a **stamp** on the envelope.

**stars:** Twinkling **stars**.

**station:** That's a train **station**.

# Ss

**stealing:** Babu Bear is **stealing** honey.

**stool:** A snake is sitting on a **stool**.

**straw:** Raju Rabbit is drinking a milkshake through a **straw**.

**strawberries:** You eat **strawberries** with cream.

a b c d e f g h i j k l m n o p q r **s** t u v w x y z

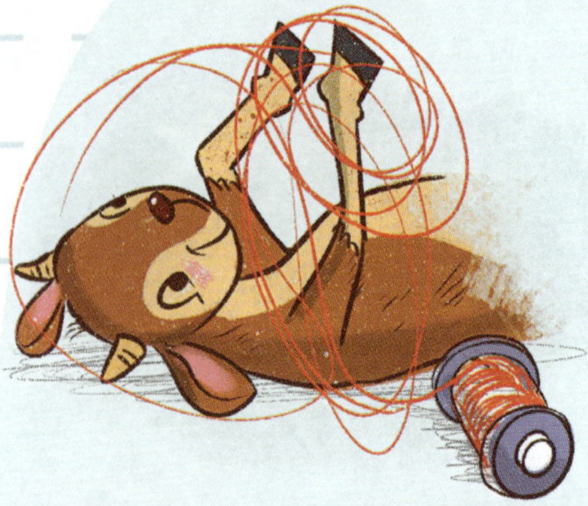

**string:** Gogo Goat is playing with the **string**.

**submarine:** A **submarine** is an underwater ship.

**sun:** A hot **sun**.

**sunglasses:** **Sunglasses** protect our eyes from the sun.

# Ss

**swan:** The **swan** has an elegant neck.

**swimming:** Tina is scared of **swimming**.

**swing:** Children love to **swing**.

**sword:** Don't be scared; that's a rubber **sword**.

# Tt

**table:** Raju Rabbit is dusting the **table**.

**tadpoles:** **Tadpoles** are baby frogs.

**tail:** Maisie Monkey has a curly **tail**.

**taxi:** Hail a **taxi**.

**teacher:** This **teacher** loves all children.

**teddy:** Coco Cat is sleeping with her **teddy** bear.

**teeth:** Raju Rabbit has lovely **teeth**.

**telephone:** Shama Sheep hears the **telephone** ring.

a b c d e f g h i j k l m n o p q r s **t** u v w x y z

**television:** Larry Lion loves watching *The Lion King* on **television**.

**tent:** The gorilla is in the **tent** in the garden.

**thief:** The **thief** is running from the police.

**thimble:** Shama Sheep is sewing with a **thimble**.

# Tt

**tie:** The little bird is wearing a red **tie**.

**throwing:** Gertrude Giraffe is **throwing** a ball into the basket.

**tiger:** Tony **Tiger** is very hungry.

**tomato:** A **tomato** is a fruit.

**toothbrush:** Dexte Dog is brushing his teeth with a **toothbrush**.

# Tt

**toothpaste:** Poppy Panda is putting **toothpaste** on her brush.

**towel:** A soft pink **towel**.

**toys:** Children love playing with **toys**.

**tractor:** Daljit Duck is learning to drive a **tractor**.

**traffic:** **Traffic** lights have three colours.

**train:** This **train** is going to France.

**tree:** This is a tall **tree**.

**tricycle:** A **tricycle** is very easy to ride.

**trousers:** Maisie Monkey is wearing a new pair of **trousers**.

**truck:** This **truck** is carrying bags of rice.

**trumpet:** Tony Tiger is playing the **trumpet**.

**trunk:** Bella the Elephant has a big **trunk**.

# Tt

**T-shirt:** The **T-shirt** is too big for the mouse.

**tulip:** **Tulips** bloom in spring.

**tunnel:** A snake lives in this **tunnel**.

**turkey:** A **turkey** trots.

# Tt

**twins:** **Twins** look alike.

**twirl:** Gertrude Giraffe did a **twirl** in front of the mirror.

# Uu

**undressing:** Farookh Frog is **undressing** to go to bed.

**umbrella:** Bashir Buffalo uses an **umbrella** in the rain.

# Vv

**vacuum:** You can easily clean your carpet with a **vacuum** cleaner.

**vegetables:** Gogo Goat loves eating **vegetables**.

abcdefghijklmnopqrstuvwxyz

# Vv

**violin:** Cathy Cow is learning to play the **violin**.

**volcano:** A **volcano** pours out very hot lava.

# Ww

**walker:** The baby loves his **walker**.

**wall:** This **wall** has a big crack.

**warm:** The river is nice and **warm**.

**wash:** You **wash** clothes in a washing machine.

**wasp:** A **wasp** is chasing Larry Lion.

a b c d e f g h i j k l m n o p q r s t u v **w** x y z

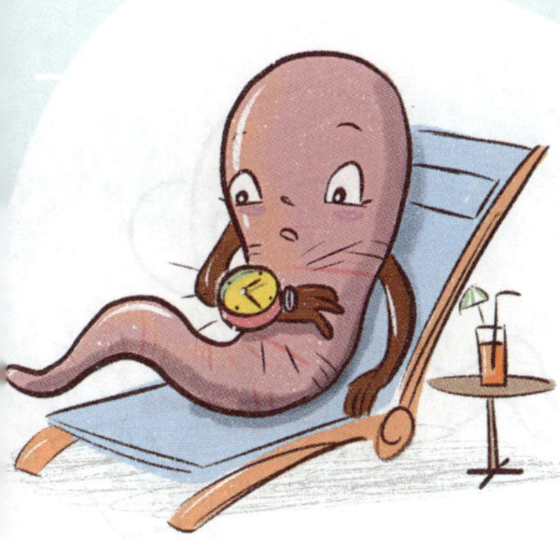

**watch:** Warner Worm is looking at his **watch**.

**whale:** That's a blue **whale**.

**wheel:** Coco Cat is rolling a **wheel**.

**whiskers:** Larry Lion has droopy **whiskers**.

# Ww

**whistle:** Cathy Cow is blowing a **whistle**.

**windmill:** Bill Bird is flying near the **windmill**.

**window:** Dexter Dog watches his neighbour from his **window**.

**witch:** A **witch** is not real.

# Ww

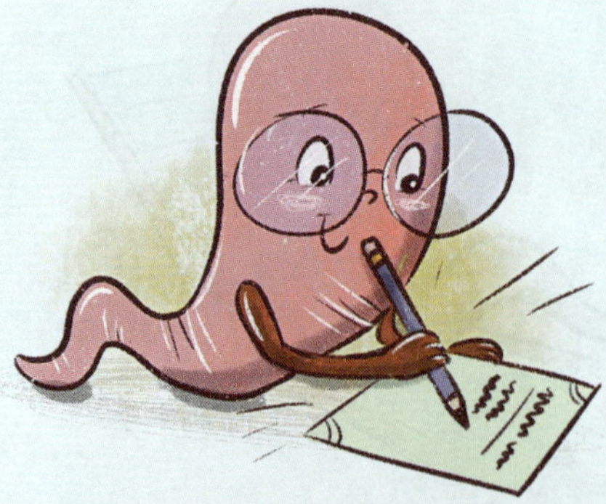

**wood:** That is enough **wood** for a fire.

**writing:** Warner Worm loves **writing**.

# Xx

**x-ray:** Bashir Buffalo has had an **x-ray** scan.

**xylophone:** This dolphin can play the **xylophone**.

# Yy

**yacht:** Daljit Duck is travelling on a **yacht**.

**yawning:** Grandma is **yawning** because she's sleepy.

# Zz

**zebra:** Zamil **Zebra** is listening to music.

**zoo:** A **zoo** is full of animals.

## Try these!

**1. Draw lines from the words** below and point to the correct objects.

A mobile phone

A newspaper

A microphone

An interactive or digital smart board

Then tell your friend what these are used for.

**2. Circle the words** to show what the boy who has hurt himself must be feeling:

pained

happy

angry

afraid

funny

What will you do if a friend or someone else you know gets hurt in front of you?

## 3. Circle the words that describe the boy and girl in the picture:

grateful grumpy brave touchy rude

## 4. Create thank-you cards

for your teachers, parents, grandparents and best friend. Here are some beautiful designs you can use.